It's Easy To Play Waltzes.

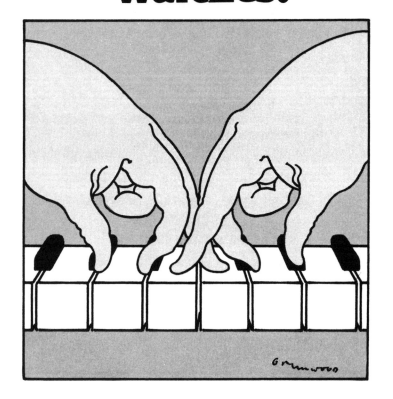

Wise Publications
London/New York/Sydney

Exclusive distributors:
Music Sales Limited
8/9 Frith Street, London W1V 5TZ
Music Sales Pty. Limited
120 Rothschild Avenue, Rosebery, NSW 2018, Australia
Music Sales Corporation
257 Park Avenue South, New York, NY 10010, U.S.A.

Waltz Of My Dreams

(A Waltz Dream)
Music by Oscar Straus. Original lyric by Ludwig Jacobson and Felix Dörmann.
English lyric by Michael Flanders.

golden, lov-ing is long, Mak-ing ev-'ry mem-o-ry one shin-ing

D6 G Gmaj7 D9 C(D sus) D7 D7+

song: Friends for the friend-less, free-dom from care, Joy that is end-less

G G+ Am D7

ritard. . . . . *poco mosso*

spark-les the air. Sad-ness and sor-row van-ish a-way, Let-ting to-

C D7 E7 Am A7 Gdim G

mor-row, wait on to-day; Life, love and laugh-ter, these are the

Fm7 D7 D7+ G D7 G C6 A7 Gdim

ritard. . . . . *molto rit.*

themes: This is Vi-en-na Waltz of my dreams.

G E7 A7 D7 C6 E♭7 G 7

Blue Danube Waltz

Johann Strauss

6.5.02

Valse Moderato

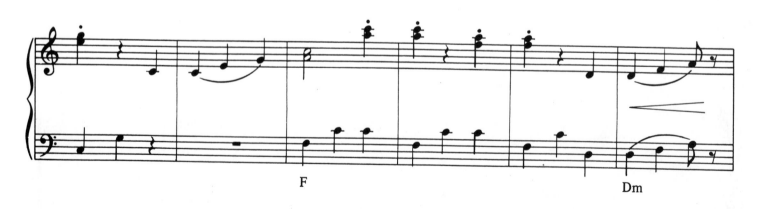

8

Waltz From "Serenade For Strings"

Peter Tchaikovsky

Over The Waves

Juventino Rosas

13

G

Gm G

E7

Am

D. S. al fine

G

14   D7   G

On My Lips Every Kiss Is Like Wine

(Waltz from 'Giuditta')

Music by Franz Lehár. Original lyric by Paul Knepler and Fritz Löhner.
English lyric by Geoffrey Dunn.

Ritard.

sist? For ev'-ry time they look at me these charms per -sist._____ But when the soft lights
danced; She held each heart en - thralled and ev'-ry eye en - tranced._____ Her spi -rit wakes in

Am   E7   Am

A tempo

glint and glance _____ As mid-night hours go by, _____ They hear me sing, they
me a - gain, _____ My for - tune wills it so. _____ At night I dance as

A7   Bb   A   Bb

Ritard.

see me dance _____ It's then that I know why. _____ } On my
she did then, _____ And this is all I know._____ } *mp*

A7   Ddim   A

Valse Moderato

lips ev' - ry kiss is like wine; _____ In my arms love is

Em7   A7   D   Em7

Ritard.   *A tempo*

more than di - vine. _____ It's en - graved in the stars high a-

A7   Bm   G   G#dim

16

bove me; _____ Men must kiss me, _____ Men must love me.

D   A7   D

_____ When my feet haun - ting rhyth-ms in - spire, _____ In my eyes gleam the

Em7   A7   D   Em7

flames of de - sire. _____ When I dance, then I know Fate's de-

A7   Bm   G   G#dim

1 *Rallentando*

sign. _____ On my lips ev' - ry kiss is like wine. _____

D   Em7   A7   D

Slower   **2** *Ritard.*

I have a   kiss is like wine.

mp

Dm   A7   D

17

Sleeping Beauty Waltz

Peter Tchaikovsky

Fine

D. C. al fine

19

Waltz in Eb

Peter Tchaikovsky

Love's Unspoken Word

(Waltz from 'The Merry Widow')
Music by Franz Lehár. Original lyric by Victor Leon and Leo Stein.
English lyric by Christopher Hassall

All the world's in love with love, and I love you.

I hear the music you. play,

It car-ries me a-way; 'All sor-row will have flown when you are mine and mine a-

lone'. So that mu-sic seems to sing. (I'm still not say-ing an-y-thing)

It's wan-ting you to know I love you so.

23

Danube Waves

Jan Ivanovici

25

Skater's Waltz

Emil Waldteufel

D.S. al fine

Waltz From "Faust"

Charles Gounod

G7

C

Fine

p

G7

C

G7

C

G7

29

C

G7

C

G7

D. C. al fine

ritard.

30   C   D7   G

Waltz Of The Flowers

(from 'Nutcracker Suite')
Peter Tchaikovsky

A7(♭5)　　　D7　　　G　　　Cdim

G　　　Cdim　　　G

Bm　　　F#7　　　Bm

F#　　　Bm　　　Bm7　　　G7　　　F#7

Bm　　　G　　　Am　　　D

32

Emperor Waltz

Johann Strauss

35

C7

F

2

F7

Bb

G7

C7

F

C9

F

G7

D. S. al fine

36

C7

F

D7(b9)

Gm

C7

F

Waltz

Johannes Brahms

I Know This Must Be Love

(Waltz from 'Count of Luxembourg')
Music by Franz Lehár. Original lyric by A. Wilner and R. Bobanzky.
English lyric by Eric Maschwitz.

One glance caught in the crowd, thrilled me through; One smile ten - der and proud, de - clared my dream-ing was true. My heart whis - pered a - loud "My love, dear love, is you." you."

F Am Bb Gm7 C

C7 D7 Bb Bbm6

F C7 F

F7 Bb Bbm6 F

C7 F F

Willow Waltz

Cyril Watters

41

Valse from Coppelia

C.P.L.Delibes

Swan Lake

Peter Tchaikovsky

Old Sleepy Head

('Schutzenliesl')
Music by Edmund Eysler. Original lyric by Carl Lindau and Leo Stein.
English lyric by Adam Carstairs.

proud of me, just wait and see; Ap - ples don't fall ve - ry
ly - ing there, so fast a - sleep. Brings back the pro - mise I

Gm7   C7

far from the tree! When I'm grown up, I shall look af - ter
said I would keep. Al - ways to be there, to stand by their

F   B♭

you, Make sure you're hap - py, that's what I shall do! } And
side; In all their trou - bles a friend and a guide.

Gm   F   Dm6   C7

slower   *ritard* *a tempo*

all my life long I'll re - mem - ber this song. Close your eyes, old

mp

Cdim   C7   Fdim   C7   F

slee - py head, troops of an - gels round your bed;

C7   Fdim F

Printed and bound in Great Britain by
Caligraving Limited Thetford Norfolk

10/97(29194)